101 Whinnying Riddles

for Horse Crazy Kids

written by **Dale Sue Wade**

drawings by **Sharon Crute**

SHARON CRUTE

contact Dale or Sharon at:
riddlesforhorsecrazykids@yahoo.com

To Pansy Bowser, whose horse stories were magical, Elaine Ream, whose support of a horse crazy kid was limitless, and Louisa Marie Goodrich, whose wild ride is just beginning.

Introduction

Do you love horses? Are you hopelessly obsessed by them? Do you think of nothing but owning your own horse or spending time with your favorite equine friend? Do you know that you will never outgrow your love of horses, no matter what anyone says??? Welcome to our world! We're glad you've joined us! Even though we're a little "long in the tooth,"* we've never stopped thinking about horses---ever!

Dale showed horses for years and shared her love of these wondrous creatures with children through camps, lessons, and clinics. Sharon took her passion for horses to the racetrack and then converted her knowledge and reverence for equine form to canvas as a celebrated equine painter.

The world of the horse is a special one, for sure. It's full of its own customs. It has its own language. To a true equine enthusiast, a leg is not a leg. It is a forearm, knee, cannon bone, ankle, fetlock, and pastern. It is a stifle, gaskin, and hock. There are hundreds of terms in everyday language that came about because of our years of dependence on horses (i.e. the term "long in the tooth").

You are about to enter that special world! In this book, you'll learn the timeless language that makes these riddles so funny---the universal language of horsemen and horsewomen! With this knowledge, you'll be more than just someone who likes horses! You'll enter the realm of the true horseperson who speaks and understands the language, and you'll have lots of laughs to share with horse people everywhere!

*The term, "long in the tooth" refers to older horses. After years spent grazing with their heads down, a horse's teeth take on a forward slant because of the effects of gravity. This gives teeth the appearance of being longer.

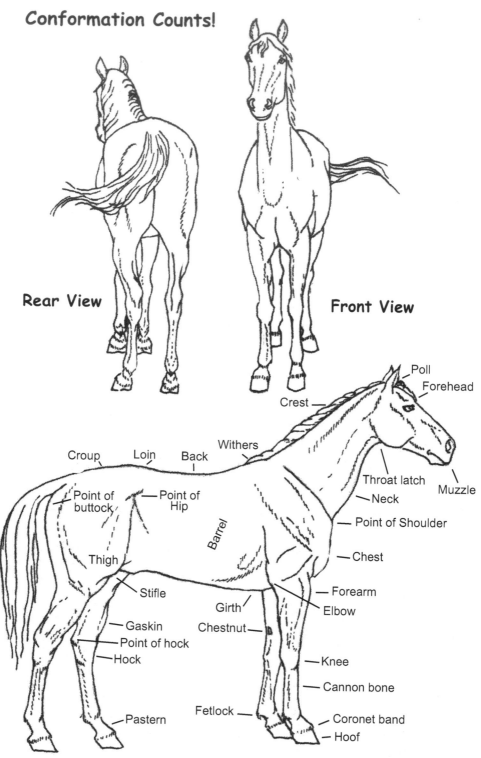

Conformation Counts!

Rear View

Front View

Poll
Forehead
Crest
Withers
Croup   Loin   Back
Throat latch
Muzzle
Neck
Point of buttock   Point of Hip
Point of Shoulder
Barrel
Chest
Thigh
Forearm
Stifle
Elbow
Girth
Gaskin
Chestnut
Point of hock
Hock
Knee
Cannon bone
Fetlock
Coronet band
Pastern
Hoof

Parts of the Horse

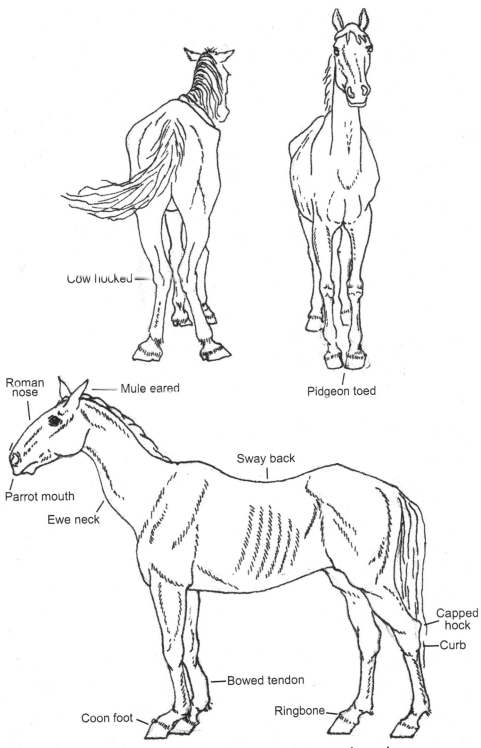

Cow hocked

Pidgeon toed

Roman nose

Mule eared

Parrot mouth

Ewe neck

Sway back

Capped hock

Curb

Bowed tendon

Ringbone

Coon foot

**Bad News! Blemishes and Unsoundness!
The Result of Poor Conformation!**

Notes

Who is New York City's favorite horse?
Why its mare, of course!

"Mayor" and "mare" are homophones. While the mayor oversees the city, a mare is a female horse over the age of four.

How does a horse measure his popularity?
With a poll.

A poll can be a survey used to measure opinions, but it is also a homonym which refers to the raised bump between a horse's ears.

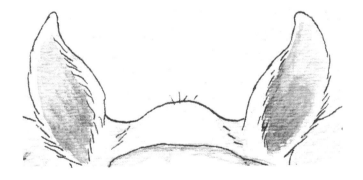

Where does a horse store his favorite beverage?
In a de-canter!!!

The canter is a three beat gait resembling a slow gallop!

What do you call a well dressed horse?
   A clotheshorse!!!

In the 1800's, the word "clotheshorse" came to refer to a
 person who loved to dress up and show off in his fancy clothes!

"The Hoss"

What did the young colt's mother do after he grew four inches?

She gave him a hand!!

Horses are not measured in inches, feet, meters, or centimeters! They are measured in hands. A hand equals four inches. A 15 hand horse is 60 inches tall. A 15.1 hand horse is 61 inches tall. A horse is never 15.5 hands. Instead, it is 16.1 hands tall (15 hands + 4 inches [which equals another hand] + a remaining inch = 16.1 hands).

What do you call a large group of horses living in the same barn?
A "neigh"borhood!

Dogs bark. Horses neigh.

What kind of rice do nine out of ten horses prefer?
Curried.

Brushing a horse is also referred to as currying a horse. There are few things that a horse likes more than being curried!

 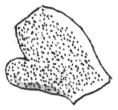

What did the banker say to the horse, who was in debt up to its knees?
You're really in hock!

The joint midway up the horse's hind leg is called his hock. It looks like his rear knee.

Where do war horses hide their ammunition?
In their cannon bone!

It's always good to know the parts of a horse's anatomy! The cannon bone is the horse's shin bone. It should be large and flat as opposed to thin and spindly. Once again, refer to the conformation chart! You'll be an expert in no time!

What happened to the horse who landed in jail while playing Monopoly?
He had to pas-a-tern.

If you've played Monopoly, you know that landing in jail means you have to pass a turn, but did you know that a pastern is an important part of the horse's lower leg? You'll find it on the conformation illustration in this book. An ideal riding horse should have a pastern positioned at a 45 degree angle. This makes for a comfortable ride!

Where do horses love to shop?
  Stall mart!

The confined area in a barn where a horse may be kept is called his stall. The average stall is about 10'x10'.

What do lady race horses wear when they go out for a night on the town?
A fur...long!

A furlong is a unit of measure utilized at horse racing tracks. It equals one- eighth of a mile.

Why did the little filly hate to brush her long hair?
Because it was a mane in the neck!

The long flowing hair on a horse's neck is called its mane.

What do you call a horse who loves the beach?
A sea horse.

The real question here is how did the sea horse get its name?
What do you think?

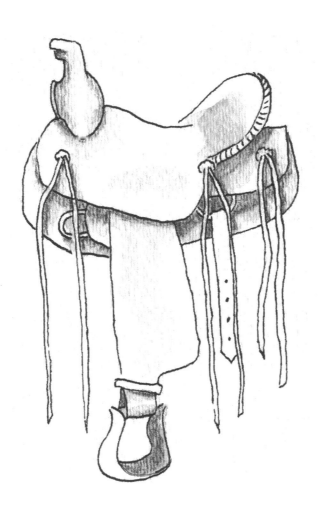

Why did the horse go to the doctor?
He had a bad colt.

A colt is a male horse less than four years of age.

What can you say about a horse who reins?
  He rules!

Cowboys like to show off the fancy moves they've taught their horses in reining contests. These amazing horses thrill crowds with fast spins and sliding stops. You could say they are the royalty of the western riding world! After all, someone has to reign over the kingdom!

How do horses send secret messages?
  With "m-horse" code.

Alfred Vail created a signal code for Samuel Morse's telegraph machine in the early 1840's. Messages could be tapped out as a series of signals representing letters.

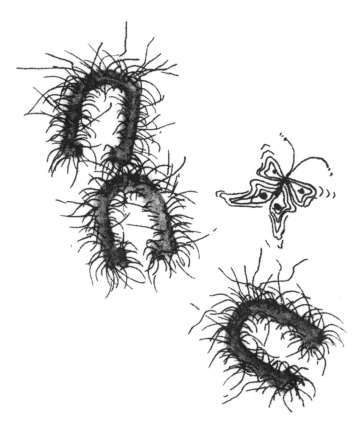

What do mother horses say when their children put off cleaning their room?
   "Stop trying to stall!"

All horses prefer a clean room, called a stall, when stabled in a barn. It should have plenty of straw or fresh shavings for bedding and be cleaned daily. Fresh water and hay should be readily available, too.

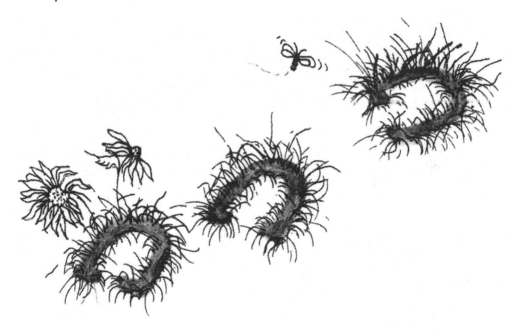

Do horses ever show up late?
   No, they hate to miss the mane event.

"Mane" and "main" are homophones. Mane refers to the hair on the crest of the horse's neck.

What do you get when you cross a horse with a train?

An iron horse.

The term "iron horse" originated around 1840 when locomotives began to take over the horse's role as a primary means of land transportation.

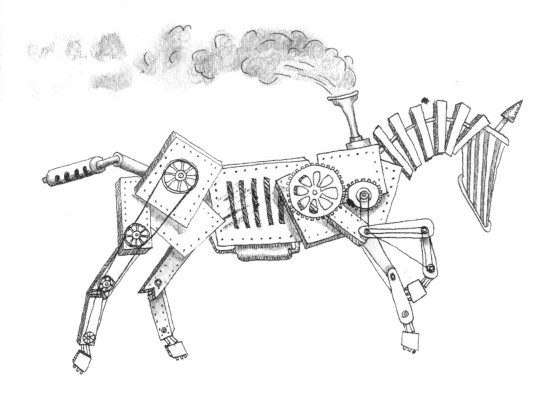

What is a mare's favorite kind of jewelry?
  A riding ring.

Many horses perform in a show ring. This is a large enclosed
area. It may or may not be under roof. Horses and riders
exhibit their skills for prizes in the show ring.

What did the filly say to the colt who tried to give her a kiss?

Don't put your "Lip-iz-an" me.

The Lipizzan or Lipizzaner horse is a beautiful, typically white horse, which is technically considered a gray. Why? These horses start out as blacks but grower lighter and lighter as they mature. The breed dates back to 1580. The Spanish Riding School of Pider, Austria has made these magnificent horses famous by showcasing them in dressage performances. Dressage is often called "ballet on horseback."

What do you say to a horse who talks too much?
  Stifle yourself!

The stifle joint is part of the horse's rear leg. It is the large joint closest to the horse's belly. Refer to the conformation chart to see the exact location!

Why did the horse cross the road?
  To get to the other stride!

Good horses travel with a long, flowing stride, no matter where they're going!

What did one colt say to the other colt?
  Let's go outside and "neigh!"

Typically, a colt is a male horse four years old or less, and they
do love to shout (neigh) and play!!

How do you make a horse fly?
Cover it with horse feathers!

Wait. What?
"Horse feathers" is a term that originated in the United States in the 1920's and means, "silliness, or nonsense." If someone tells you something that is difficult to believe, you can say, "That's a bunch of horse feathers!"

What kind of car do 99% of horses prefer?
A mustang!

The Ford motor company named their famous Mustang car after the wild mustang horses that live in the western United States!

What do you call a filly who wins an election?
Mare!

A female horse older than four years is a mare. If she is less than four, she is considered a filly. A horse must be 18 to vote (just kidding).

   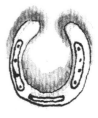

Where do mini horses play golf?
At a miniature golf course!

One of the smallest miniature horses ever was Bond Tiny Tim. He was only 19 inches tall at his withers (4.3 hands). It is unknown whether he was a golfer. Mini horses are now used as guide animals for humans.

What do you call a group of horses on in-line skates?
A roller derby!

What a thrilling sight that would be! Even so, it couldn't compete with the excitement of some of the world's most famous horse races, like Britain's Epsom Derby, the Kentucky Derby, and the Santa Anita Derby in California.

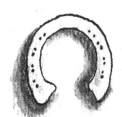   

How does a horse start his engine?
With a joc-key

Jockeys are the people partners on the backs of those incredible race horses!

Why did the horse have to stay after school?
He couldn't resist the teacher's apple!

Long associated with teachers and education, the apple is a favorite treat of any horse! That must be why horses are so smart!

I will not bite into the
I will not bite into the
I will not bite into the
I will not bite into the
I will not bite into the
I will not bite into the
I will not bite into the
I will not bite into the
will not bite into the
not bite into the
MY FRIEND FLICKA
SEABISCUIT
ERACER

What is it called when a horse puts his elbows on the table?

Poor s-table manners!

Even horses must have good manners!

Why was the horse so smart?

He ate a lot of brain grain.

Just remember, you are what you eat!

What do you call a horse who earns an Olympic Gold Medal?
A "whinnier!"

When a horse shouts for joy, it's called a whinny. If you won a gold medal, you'd whinny, too!

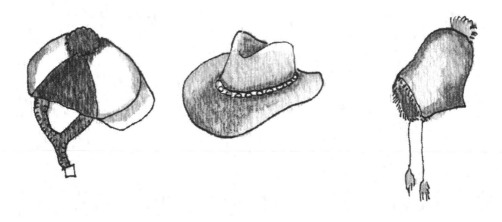

Can you guess a horse's favorite bee?
The Kentucky Der-bee.

The Kentucky Derby is without a doubt the most famous horse race in North America. It is run on the first Saturday of May each year in Louisville, Kentucky. The first meet took place in May 17, 1875 and was won by a colt named Aristides. Arisitides was ridden to victoryby Oliver Lewis. He was trained by Ansel Williamson.

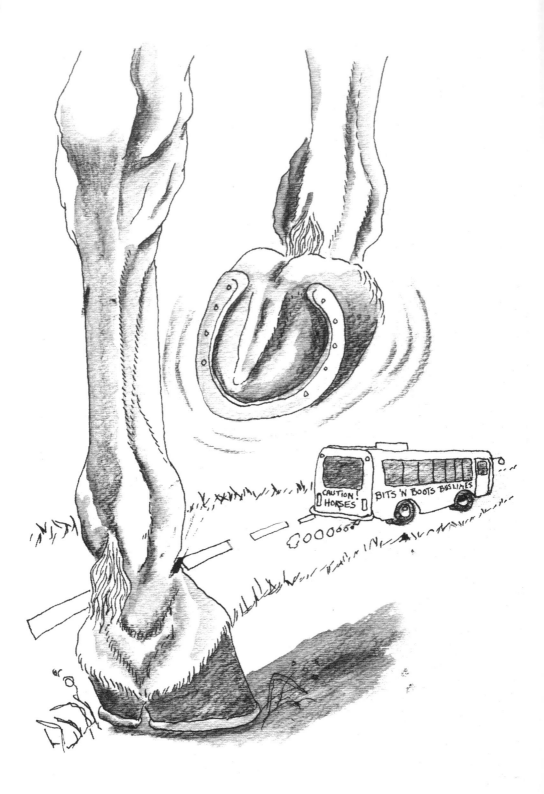

What did the horse say when he missed the bus?
Guess I'll just have to "hoof it."

The common expression, "hoofing it," refers to walking. A horse's feet are called hooves.

What did the cowboy say to his parrot as it prepared to ride his horse?

Polly wanna' tack her?

Tack refers to the equipment worn by a horse. If you tack up a horse, you put the saddle and bridle on the horse.

What do you get when you cross Benedict Arnold with a horse?

A horse traitor.

Benedict Arnold was born in Connecticut and was a general in the American Continental Army during the Revolutionary War. He changed sides during the war and fought for the British. He was a traitor. Naturally, this made the Americans very angry. His name has gone down in history to mean someone who is disloyal and sneaky.

On the other hand, someone who buys and sells horses for a living is called a horse trader. Unfortunately, the term "horse trader" can sometimes refer to a person who is not entirely honest in his dealing, either.

What did the jockey ask the baker?
   Do you have a hearty, thorough, bread?

Have you heard of the Kentucky Derby? It is arguably one of the most famous horse races in the world. The only breed eligible to compete in this prestigious race is the Thoroughbred. Every jockey, or rider, in the race longs for a magnificent, strong steed!

Why do horses make good writers?
   Because they like to "plot" along.

Walking slowly is plodding, although no one likes to read a book with a slow story, or plot!

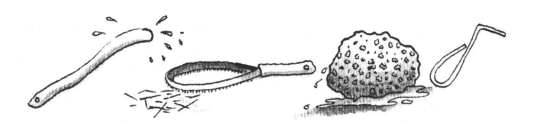

Why wouldn't the farmer allow the horse near his pond?

Because the horse always walked on his frogs.

The frog is located on the underside of the horse's hoof. It is v-shaped and acts as somewhat of a shock absorber for the hoof. It also pumps blood up the horse's leg every time the hoof hits the ground. That's a lot of work for one frog!

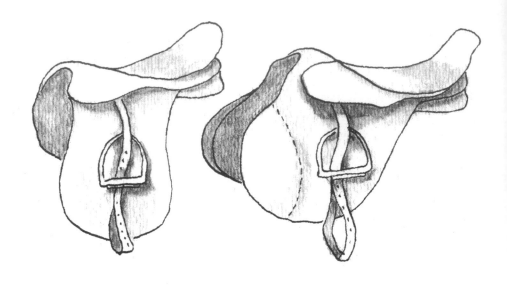

Why aren't horses good cooks?
Because they never remember to "stirrup" the food.

The saddle, which is placed on the horse's back for the rider to sit in, has a stirrup on each side. The rider places her feet in the stirrups.

What kind of horse makes the best president?
One who always takes the correct lead.

When running, which is known as cantering or galloping, the horse leads with either his left front leg or his right front leg and the opposite diagonal hind leg. To be most efficiently balanced, the horse's lead should follow the direction he is going in (i.e. when traveling in an arc to the left, the horse should be on his left lead).

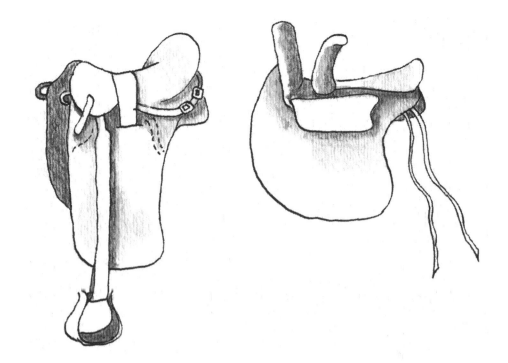

Why did the dentist scream in terror when he opened the horse's mouth?
   He saw wolf teeth!

That would be shocking! But did you know that horses actually have some small teeth referred to as wolf teeth?

What kind of horses make the best friends?
   Palominos.

Who wouldn't want a beautiful golden palomino with a silky white mane and a flowing white tail for a pal?

How did the horse orbit the earth?
  In a "saddle-lite."

The saddle is the piece of equipment on which the rider is seated.

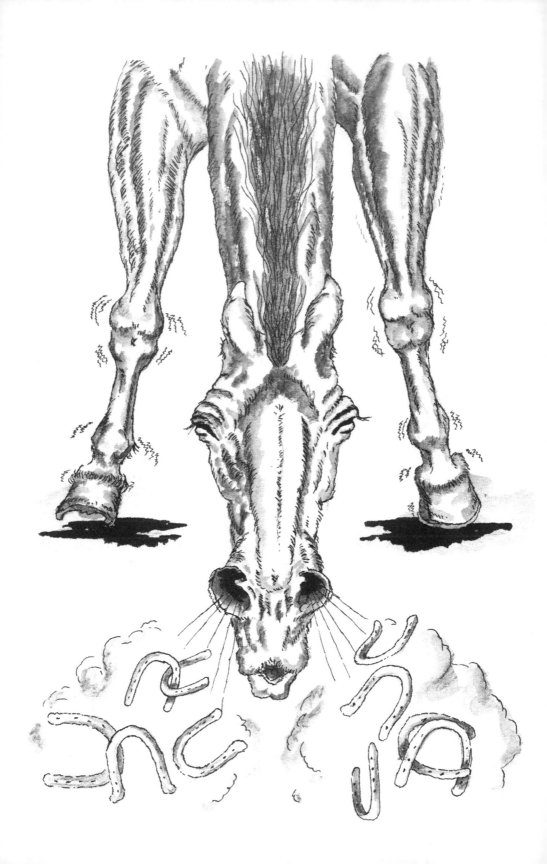

What do horses say when they sneeze?
  "Horse-SHOE!!!"

Yes, horses wear shoes, too! They are thin metal plates that are attached to the bottom of the horse's hoof.

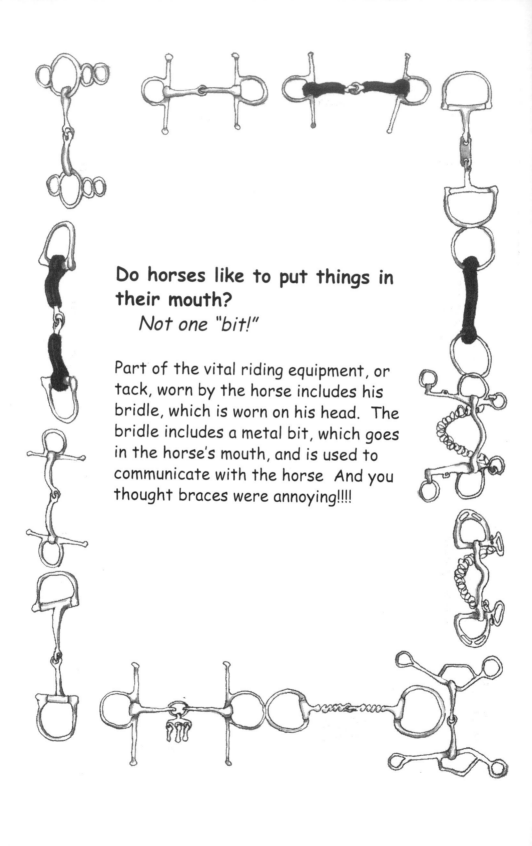

Do horses like to put things in their mouth?
Not one "bit!"

Part of the vital riding equipment, or tack, worn by the horse includes his bridle, which is worn on his head. The bridle includes a metal bit, which goes in the horse's mouth, and is used to communicate with the horse And you thought braces were annoying!!!!

A busy horse who spends her time running in circles can often be heard saying this to her friends...
   Let's do "lunge" some day!

A popular training technique is called "lungeing." The horse carries out the trainer's commands as he circles her while attached to a long rope.

What did George Washington say to his blacksmith?
   See you at Valley Forge!

The blacksmith is responsible for shaping metal horse shoes to fit each horse. He does this by heating the metal at his forge until it can be bent and twisted with metal tongs and a hammer.

George Washington, the first president of the United States, spent one of the longest winters of his life at Valley Forge, Pennsylvania gearing up to continue his battle with the British.

History tells us that Washington was quite a horseman and loved to parade around on his striking white horse, Nelson.

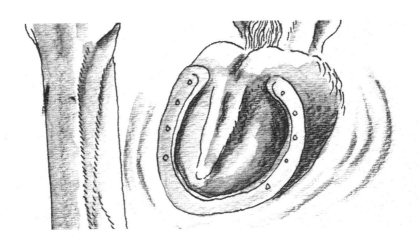

What is a horse's favorite pie?
   Shoofly pie.

Flies can be real pests to horses! You can bet that when the flies are buzzing, the horses are saying, "Shoo! Get out! Get lost!" Interestingly enough, there really is a pie called Shoofly Pie. Its main ingredient is molasses, a popular ingredient in horse feed. Ummmm.

How does a horse feel when he loses a race?
  Disg-raced!

Are horses really competitive? Sure they are! Some horses refuse to bring up the rear while running in the pasture and will warn other horses to stay out of their way with a toss of their head and a swish of their tail!

The legendary race horse, Seabiscuit, supposedly stared down his rival, War Admiral, during their epic match race at Pimlico Race Course in 1938, causing War Admiral to relent.

How did the horse buy his new barn?
  On the inSTALLment plan!

Barns come in all price ranges, from fancy to frugal. The horse who wants to live in a four star stall may want to consider paying for it month by month, on the installment plan!

What do you call a horse who likes to eat on the run?

A galloping gourmet!

More like run to eat! Mealtime is a favorite time of day for horses! It's important to feed them at scheduled times and stick to the plan.

What do you call a horse who has a bad dream in July?

A mid-summer's night mare.

That famous playwright, William Shakespeare, wrote "A Midsummer Night's Dream," and while it's not about a horse, Shakespeare clearly understood people who are passionate about horses. He penned the famous words, "A horse! A horse! My kingdom for a horse!"

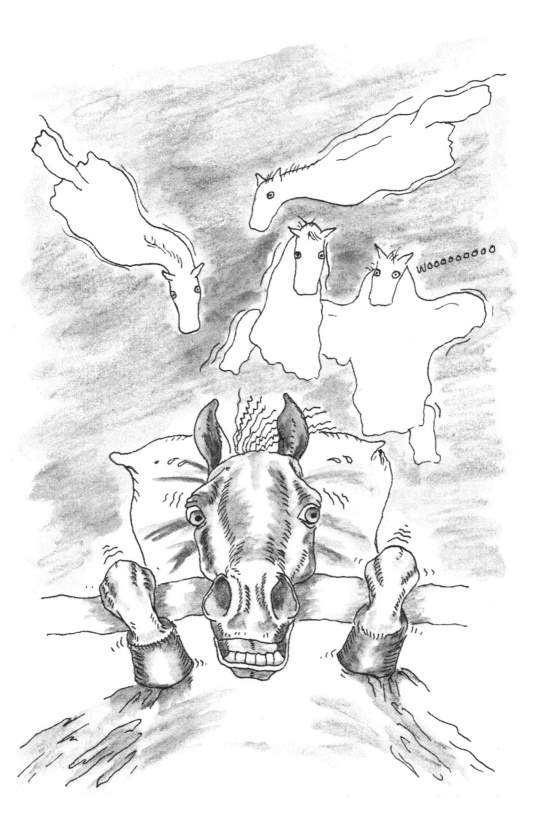

Why is it so hard to stop a group of galloping horses?
   Because they're "heard" of hearing!

Yep, another homophone!
A herd of horses is like a gaggle of geese is like a pack of dogs is like a flock of pigeons... Hey....I heard that comment!

Who do horses visit for an eye exam?
   A "see horse."

Because a horse's eye is located on each side of his head, he has a panoramic view of the area around him!

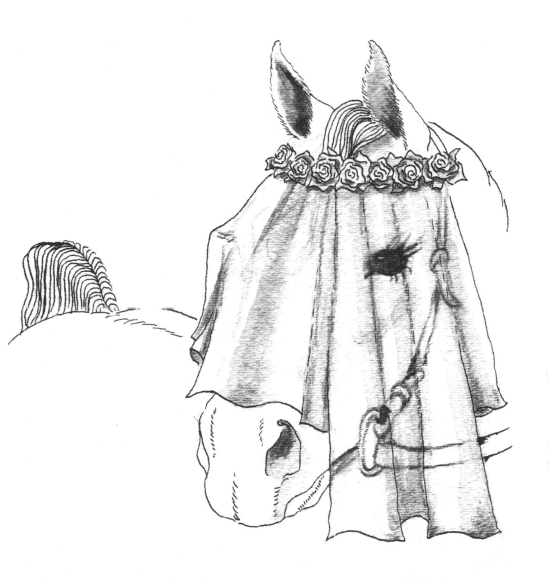

What did the mare wear over her face on her wedding day?

A "bridle" veil.

A bridle is the piece of equipment, or tack, on the horse's head when he is being ridden or driven in a cart. A bride to be wears her bridal veil on her wedding day.

What did the big horse use to clear a giant jump?
   He used a lot of fours!

The world record for jumping was set by a Thoroughbred horse born in Chile originally named "Faithful." He retired from racing in 1944 and began a new career with the Chilean Cavalry School. When his tremendous jumping ability was discovered, his name was changed to "Huaso," meaning "cowboy" in Spanish.

On February 5, 1949 at the show grounds of Vina Del Mar in Chile, Huaso defeated rival Chileno and jumped 8 feet 1 and 1/4inches (2.47 meters) to establish the world record. Needless to say, a lot of force was required for take -off, and a lot of force was met upon landing!

What kind of horse does Picasso prefer?
   A paint!

The American Paint Horse is a spotted horse with Quarter Horse or Thoroughbred bloodlines. Famed artist, Pablo Picasso, would have surely found them fun to draw!

What did one horse say to the other horse when he snatched his treat?

I thought you "carrot" about me!

Carrots rank among a horse's favorite treats!

Did the pony walk or ride the bus home from school?

He always rodeoed.

Rodeos are popular events for cowboys to show off their skills!

What do you call it when a horse won't stop talking?

A long winded "disc-horse."

It's easy to listen to a lengthy discourse if it's about a favorite topic---like horses!

Why did the horse hurry through his treats?

Because he didn't have "apple" time to eat!

Even if given ample time to eat, most horses still eat quickly, especially when enjoying delicious treats like apples.

Why should you never look a gift horse in the mouth?

Because you might not like what he presents!

A horse's age can be estimated by examining his teeth. Sometimes it's best not to know, just graciously accept the present!

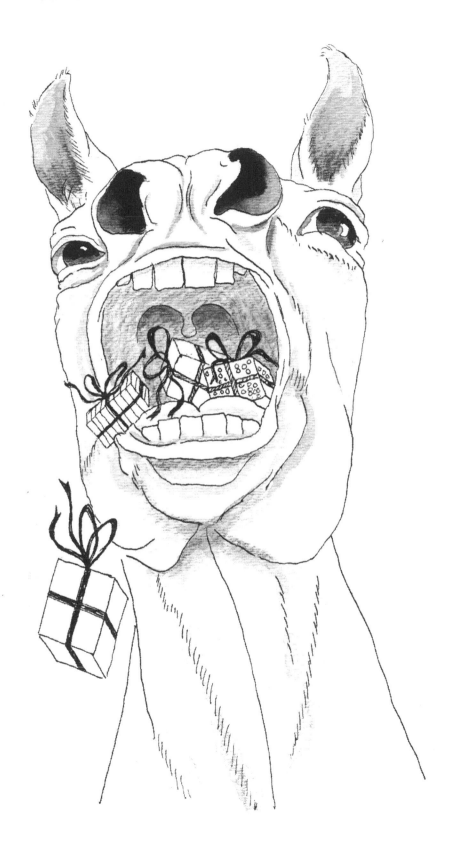

What is a horse's favorite side dish?
  Pinto beans!

Pinto horses have beautifully spotted coats.

What did the witch say to the horse before she changed him into a frog?
   Time to change your saddle pad for a lily pad!

Before a saddle is situated on the horse's back, a saddle pad is placed there. You could say it's the equivalent of horsey underwear!

Where is a horse's favorite place to trade?
   The stock market.

Horses fit the category of livestock (cows, pigs, goats, etc.) and are sometimes bought and sold at stock markets. You won't find one on Wall Street!

What do horses put on pancakes?
Their favorite stirrup.

The rider places her foot in the stirrups of the saddle. Hopefully, they're not sticky.

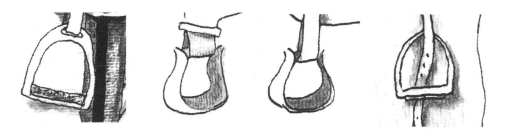

Why did the horse join the army?
He wanted to be the next Man O' War.

Man O' War is a legendary race horse who was born on March 29, 1917. He is considered by many to have been the greatest race horse of all time. His owner, Samuel Riddle was once offered a million dollars for Man O' War. He is said to have retorted, " Lots of men have a million dollars, but only one can own Man O' War."

Man O' War died on November 1, 1947 of a heart attack. His funeral was broadcast over the radio, and more than 2,000 grief stricken people attended the memorial of the beloved horse. He is buried at the Kentucky Horse Park in Lexington Kentucky.

How can you recognize a really great horse?
He is outstanding in his field!

A beautiful horse in a peaceful pasture field is a lovely sight, indeed!

What kind of jokes do horses like?
Corny ones!

Corn is a favorite food of horses!

What do you call a horse who plays violin?
Fiddler on the hoof.

Better a fiddler on the hoof than a horse on the roof!

Which horses make the worst gardeners?
  The ones who Run for the Roses!

That famous American horse race, the Kentucky Derby, is known as The Run for the Roses. This is because only the winner of the race is adorned with a blanket of roses over his shoulders.

Which horses make the best musicians?
The ones who are good, and sound!

Musicians have to have a good sound, and a good horse must be sound! Horsemen use the term, "sound," to refer to a healthy horse!

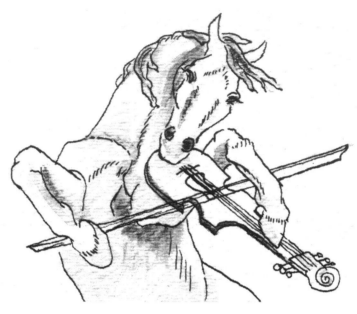

Why do horses like to get treats?
Because they have big "apple-tites."

 Even a delicious apple will only go a little way in satisfying a horse's big appetite!

What did one horse say to the other when they met in a snowstorm?

Aren't you Fresian?

The Friesian horse is a majestic equine breed that originated in the Friesland region of the Netherlands. Black in color with flowing manes and tails, they appear in pictures painted by the Old Dutch Masters carrying knights into battle.

What kind of horse makes the best quarterback?
  A Paso Fino.

Actually, the Paso Fino is not known for its fine passing
 abilities, either. Instead, it is known for its fine pace, or gait.
This small, but hearty horse was developed in Puerto Rico and
South America during the 16th-century from Spanish horses
brought to the Americas by the Spanish conquistadors. They
have a distinct stride, the paso corto, which is equivalent to a
trot, but much smoother and easier for the rider to sit.
Aaaahhhhh.

What kind of horse makes the worst quarterback?
  A half-flinger.

Okay, so the Haflinger breed may not be able to throw a ball
very far, but it is a versatile breed that can be used for riding
or driving in a cart. The breed is said to have originated in the
Austrian Tyrol. Small and tough, it is a sturdy mountain breed
known for being strong, surefooted, and intelligent.

What do you get if a horse steps on your toe?
   A "pent-toe."

Nothing worse than a toe pent under a horse's hoof! Ooowww! It will be bruised and spotted for days. Remember the earlier reference to the spotted horse known as a pinto? Aaargh...the joke is painful, too!

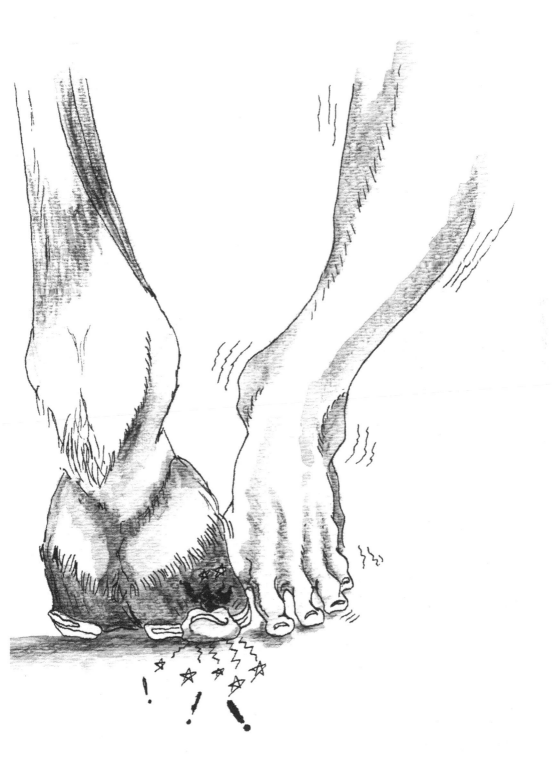

What was the real reason Napoleon was dethroned?
He tried to "Selle Francais."

The Selle-Francais, which means French Saddle Horse, was developed in France during the 19th- century. These horses are incredibly athletic and are often seen in jumping competitions.

The legendary 19th-century emperor of France, Napoleon Bonaparte, tried to conquer most of Europe, but lucky for the French (Francais) he never did try to sell France. He did, however, sell a huge chunk of land to the United States. A deal at only three cents an acre, this land sale was known as the Louisiana Purchase.

What kind of horse prefers a U-Haul to a horse trailer?
A Gypsy Vanner.

The Gypsy Vanner is a new breed of horse that was imported to the United States. It represents the finest characteristics of selectively bred European Gypsy cart horses and is able to pull a heavy wagon.

Horses are normally transported over long distances in a horse trailer or horse van. Transporting horses by foot the old fashioned way would make for a long haul!

Why did the horse turn the politician out to pasture?

Because he was an old gray mayor.

Older horses are often allowed to retire and relax in a nice green pasture. This is referred to as turning a horse out to pasture and has become an idiom, or a colorful way of referring to something, which is in this case, retirement.

Mayor and mare are homophones. The first rules the city; the second is a female horse older than four years.

What does a rodeo rider slip into before he performs?

His "buck-skin."

Rodeo riders often compete to see who can stay on a bucking horse. Wow! Good luck with that!

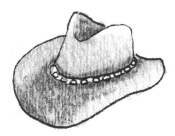

What is a horse's best friend when he jumps from an airplane?
   A Parelli-chute.

When was the last time you saw a horse jump from a plane? Never, right? Well, if you were to see a horse dive from a plane, chances are he would have been trained by someone like Pat Parelli, a popular teacher of Natural Horsemanship. He encourages people to think like a horse when training horses to perform to their highest potential.

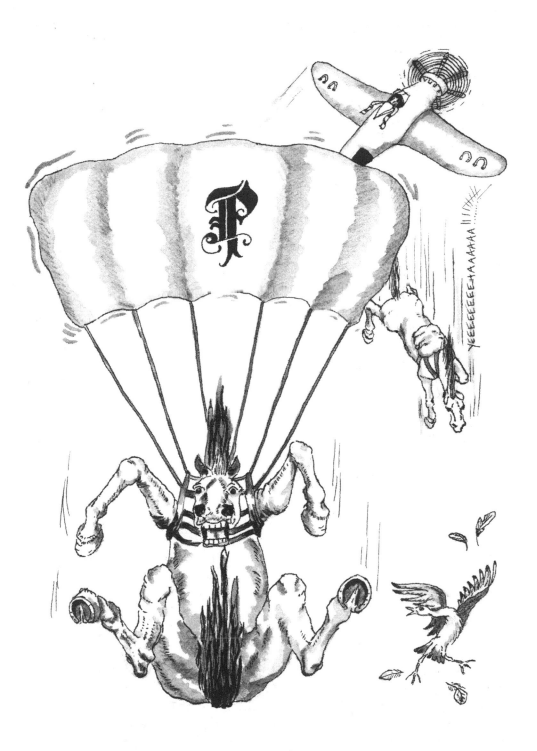

Who is in charge of the tooth fairy, the good fairy, and the fairy godmother?
   The farrier!

The farrier is the person whose job it is to trim and care for the horses hooves each month.

What do you call a wise-cracking horse who refuses to wear a bridle?
   "Bosal the Clown!"

A bosal is a hardened hoop of leather that goes around a horse's nose. It is used on a bridle in place of a bit to give the rider a tool with which to control and communicate with the horse.

What kind of musical group do horses enjoy most?
A coronet band.

The coronet band is a thin line of white tissue at the top of the horse's hoof.

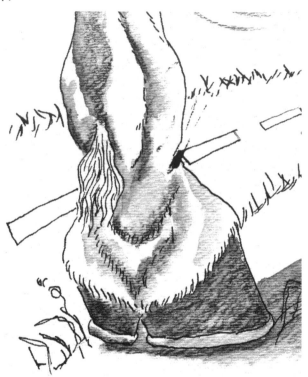

Where do horses like to entertain?
Their saddle pad!

Pad, digs, crib, hizzy, spot, and spread...these are all slang words for a house or home.

The saddle pad is essential equipment for making the horse comfortable while carrying the saddle. It can help to properly balance the saddle, thus making the rider feel more at home on the horse's back.

What kind of dressing do cow ponies prefer on their salads?
 Ranch.

What kind did you think he liked? Bleu cheese?

What do you call a rider crossing a creek while riding her horse bareback?

Up a creek without a saddle!

Better to be up a creek without a saddle than up a creek without a paddle!

What do you call a cowboy with a stick?

A cowpoke!

A cowpoke is too busy doing ranch work to play with sticks!

How can you tell if a horse has a big ego?
He has an overly inflated sense of self-girth.

The girth is the term used to refer to the circumference of a horse just behind his withers and front legs. It is also a piece of equipment similar to a wide belt that is attached to the saddle. It goes around the horse's girth to hold the saddle in place.

What do you call a cowboy being drug by his horse alongside of the road?
   A Cinder-fella?

Ouch! Nothing worse than being pulled across tiny stones!

Why do horses love salad bars?
   They're crazy about hoof dressing!

Horses often need hoof dressing to keep their hooves healthy (think hand cream for humans).

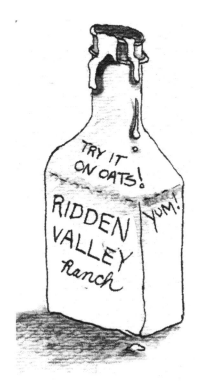

Where do horses go to shop?
   Filly-delphia.

Remember, a filly is a female horse four years old or younger.

What do you get if you go trick-or-treating at a horse's house?
   A candy dapple.

A dapple is the term used to describe the quarter-sized spots that are just slightly darker than the horse's coat color.

What do you call a cowboy who falls off his horse every time he gallops over a small hill?
  Humpty- dumpty!

A few riding lessons never hurt anyone, but falling off a horse has!

How did the Indian pony find his way around Indiana?

He used his Indian atlas.

I'll bet he went to Indianapolis!

What is a must if you throw a dinner party for a horse?
   A stable and mares!

And don't forget the table and chairs!

Why did the Cavalry horse go to the psychiatrist?
   He needed to get things sworded out!

The Cavalry was the military division that used horses in warfare. Soldiers wore swords as part of their equipment. Talk about stressful!

What do you call a sheep who directs traffic while riding a horse?

A mounted fleece-man!

Many cities employ mounted policemen to patrol their streets.

Where did the cowboy land when he was thrown from the bucking machine?

Floor-duh!

Mechanical horses are sometimes used to teach riders how to sit a bucking bronco. There's only one place to land when thrown!

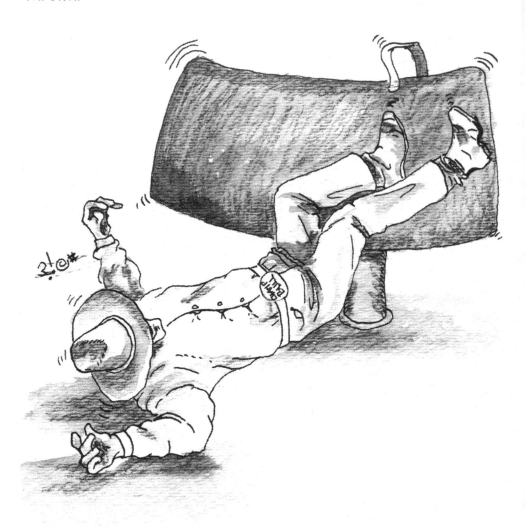

What kind of magic do horses practice?
S-horsery!

You have to admit there is something magical about horses!

Why did the roping horse head west?
He wanted to see Cow-la-fornia!

Roping horses are ridden by cowboys and have been trained to work with cowboys as they lasso cattle with ropes.

What kind of race requires a horse to be limber, fly over timber, and yet leave wings on the ground?
   A steeplechase race!

A steeplechase is a type of horse race in which horses jump over obstacles. It can take place on a race track or across open country. In 18th-century Ireland where the races originated, riders would race their horses from church steeple to church steeple, clearing ditches, walls, and fences as they went.

Today there are two forms of steeplechasing---hurdle and timber. Hurdle events take place at race tracks and steeplechase meets. Horses jump standardized fences of 52 inches while running 2 to 3 miles.

Timber races are generally three to four miles long and are not held at any major US tracks but instead take place at steeplechase meets. This is because the solid fences are immovable. Just ask any horse and rider who fail to clear them!

The most famous timber race is the English Grand National. It gained notoriety as the setting for the film, "National Velvet." The Breeder's Cup Grand National Steeplechase (formerly the American Grand National) in Fair Hill, New Jersey is the richest event in American steeplechasing.

What was the first question asked by the ancient Roman horse when he arrived in town?

'Sara-toga store around here?

While togas were considered fashionable clothing among ancient Romans, it's unlikely that they could compete with the stylish attire found at Saratoga Springs, New York, where the hottest horses in racing (and their owners) come for a cool summer.

Made in the USA
Charleston, SC
01 July 2012